T0165598

His Love Endures Forever

Constance Shultes

BALBOA.
PRESS
A DIVISION OF HAY HOUSE

Balboa Press books may be ordered through booksellers or by contacting:

Balboa Press
A Division of Hay House
1663 Liberty Drive
Bloomington, IN 47403
www.balboapress.com
1-(877) 407-4847

Because of the dynamic nature of the Internet, any web addresses or links contained in this book may have changed since publication and may no longer be valid. The views expressed in this work are solely those of the author and do not necessarily reflect the views of the publisher, and the publisher hereby disclaims any responsibility for them.

The author of this book does not dispense medical advice or prescribe the use of any technique as a form of treatment for physical, emotional, or medical problems without the advice of a physician, either directly or indirectly. The intent of the author is only to offer information of a general nature to help you in your quest for emotional and spiritual well-being. In the event you use any of the information in this book for yourself, which is your constitutional right, the author and the publisher assume no responsibility for your actions.

Any people depicted in stock imagery provided by Thinkstock are models, and such images are being used for illustrative purposes only. Certain stock imagery © Thinkstock.

ISBN: 978-1-4525-4274-4 (sc)
ISBN: 978-1-4525-4273-7 (e)

Library of Congress Control Number: 2011960698

Printed in the United States of America

Balboa Press rev. date: 11/14/2011

To Scott, Mark, Juli, Max, Natalie, Sierra, Charlie, and to all of God's children.

Chapter 1

"**D**o you know you are going to die someday?"

I was surprised to hear this question from my friend. I was only eight years old at the time, and I felt I would live forever.

Here it was, a lovely summer day, and we were in our favorite spot in my backyard, under the grapevine, which was covered with grapes. Elly was reaching up for another bunch of purple grapes. "Yes," she went on, her big, brown eyes looking into my blue ones. "It will happen, and you should think about such things."

I wondered how well-versed she was in these matters, as she was two years older than I and attended a religious school. We did not attend church or even own a Bible. My parents rarely discussed religion.

It was 1940, and the sky was blue, the sun a rich, buttery yellow. Today, the sun seems a lighter yellow. Could the scientists be right, and the sun may be burning itself out?

I had yet to answer Elly's question. When her mother's stern voice called her home, she arose and was gone in a flash.

I sat on the grass, thinking about what Elly had said, and I decided to go in search of my mother. I found her in the kitchen. She had washed the curtains and had them drying on a wooden platform called a curtain stretcher. It had pins around the edges and held the curtains in place until they dried. She was now washing the windows, and the sun coming in was adding golden highlights to her soft, brown hair.

I remember our house always sparkled; my mother seemed to enjoy housecleaning very much. I think she liked it better than cooking, as I don't remember many of her dishes that I loved. I was very thin and not interested in food, which was a worry for her.

As I called to my mother, she looked up at me with her sparkling, green eyes and that beautiful, white smile that I loved so much. "Mother, am I going to die?"

She was startled by my question and asked who I had been discussing such things with. I explained about my conversation with Elly under the grapevine.

My mother took me onto her lap and said, "You are not to worry. It will only happen when you are very, very old, and by then, you won't even care, because you will have lived many, many years and be very, very tired." When we heard a group of friends starting a game of hide and seek, my mother gave me a loving shove and said, "Now go and join your friends."

Traffic was slow on our unpaved dead-end street. I went outside in a happy frame of mind to see a group of friends gathered around the iceman's open-bed truck. He had gone into a house to deliver a large, fifty-cent piece of ice. To receive ice, a family would put a card in their window denoting which size of ice they wanted.

When he was gone, we would jump up onto the truck to gather small pieces of ice to place in our mouths. It felt so cool on a hot summer day. With no refrigerators, the ice was very important for our iceboxes. The icebox held a large pan underneath to catch the melted water. We needed to empty it often before the pan overflowed—which it sometimes did!

The young man came back out of the house holding his large ice tongs and yelling at us kids to get off of his truck. We found this very fun and exciting.

When the "rag man" came down our street, we were a little leery. He was an old man and not friendly. He came down our street with a horse and wagon, calling, "Any rags for sale?" He stopped when someone came outside with bundles of old clothes and other materials. I heard he made rag carpets out of the rags he bought. Some of the mothers would remind us to be good or we could be sold too.

We could hear the "soap box operas" coming from the open windows. Our mothers had the radios on as they worked. We heard *Ma Perkins, Just Plain Bill, Amos and Andy,* and *Our Gal Sunday,* stories that continued each day and kept our mothers interested.

With friends and relatives living in the vicinity, we had people stop by often. We had no telephones to call and see if the time was appropriate; we were just happy to see them, no appointment necessary.

Chapter 2

We had quite an extended family, so I didn't mind too much being an only child, although I would have liked a brother or sister. Occasionally we would have a relative move in with us for a time if he or she was in a financial bind.

My father's stepmother lived with us, but to be precise, we actually lived with her, as the house was left to her after the death of my grandfather. It became ours upon the death of my beloved Bobka, as I called her. She had raised three children after their mother died and she had married my grandfather. She was the only mother they knew.

Bobka was Roman Catholic, and she often sat with a string of wooden beads she called rosary beads and whispered to herself as she held each bead. I found this most fascinating—she said a prayer on each bead.

My maternal grandparents were Seventh-Day Adventists. Occasionally I would attend services with them, which were held in a large farmhouse. The grounds were home to many milk cows. On Sundays, they took out all of the furniture from the living room. The minister would set up chairs and the organ, which his wife played. I loved to sing, and I enjoyed the hymns. This was the extent of my religious training.

My parents being agnostic, my mother only taught me one thing: never to lie. If she doubted something I had said, she would tell me to hold up my right hand to God to swear what I had said was true. This I would never do if I had lied. I never knew what would happen to me, but I suspected I would be struck by lightning.

My mother loved to tell stories of her childhood. She had six siblings: four brothers and two sisters. They lived on a farm in Pennsylvania, which brought many adventures. The "bee adventure" I found particularly intriguing. The seven siblings had all gone out to the meadow to play and found a beehive in a tree. After observing the bees go from flower to flower, my mother had an idea. As second oldest, she had their attention, and she whispered to the others, "Let's break it," meaning the beehive. Before anyone could even think of looking for a rock big enough, one large bee flew right at her. The bee went right to her face, and the sting was on her nose. They all ran home with their screaming sister. My mother's motto became "Never underestimate the intelligence of any creature."

For me, school plays were exciting. We did one each year, held at our large high school, though we were in grade school. We performed *The Wedding of Tom Thumb*. A tiny boy from first grade and a big, beautiful sixth-grade girl were the bride and groom. The guest list included elegantly dressed friends of mine representing certain movie stars. I was just a flower girl and not as lovely as the other flower girl. She had long, golden curls to her waist and received a gasp from the audience. It proved to me that my mother had cut my dull, brown hair much too short.

The following year, when they picked dancers for *The Glow-Worm*, I was home sick with the chicken pox. What luck! When I got better and went back to school, I found I would be in a singing group. We were dressed in red, white, and blue and held a cardboard axe while we sang about George Washington cutting down the cherry tree. Some fun! I wished I could dance the Glow-Worm.

One day, the teacher asked me if I would also dance with the Glow-Worms. It seems an argument with a parent made one girl drop out. My mother took over the costume and altered it to fit me. It was beautiful, soft yellow covered in sparkling sequins. We danced to the music, "Glow, little glow-worm, glitter, glitter." Because I was in the first "Washington" song, the teacher had to rush me backstage to change costumes. I was a star!

Chapter 3

Not being a large city, our town had few streetlights. That made it very dark at night, displaying a night sky full of bright stars. One clear, cloudless night, my mother spread a blanket out on our soft grass in our backyard. She had invited one of my friends to come over and stargaze with me. We were all alone, and the sky was very big and bright. It is a night that I will always remember.

A million sparkling stars gazed down on us. My friend, who was a few years older than I, pointed out the Milky Way and the Big and Little Dipper; it was extremely beautiful. We saw what my friend called a falling star as the light blazed across the heavens. It made me wonder who made such a beautiful universe.

When my mother came back out, she told me to wish on a bright star, and maybe my wish might come true. It was time to come back inside, but we had been very intrigued for the hour we had spent alone in the darkness. How mysterious it had been, and wishing on a star did indeed bring forth the red two-wheeler bicycle I had been hoping for.

With winter came sledding down a nearby hill and ice-skating on a frozen pond near our home. Sonja Henie was the Olympic gold medal skater of our time. Blonde and beautiful, she made movies that we loved.

How easy life was for me. How could I know the changes that were to come? It began as my mother found a lump under her left armpit. What could that be? The doctor called it a swollen gland but recommended it be removed. We were worried as she entered the hospital for its removal. She spent a week in the hospital, and when she came home, we hoped the worst was over.

Chapter 4

*O*ne summer day in 1941, my friends had a new game. They called it "I Declare War." They had drawn a huge square in the dirt and divided it into countries. We each had to pick a country and put one foot in our chosen country. When the leader of the game called out, "I declare war," we were to run as fast as we could, because she had a small stick. When she called "stop," the one closest to her would be hit with the stick, and it happened to be me. I waited in excitement to see what would happen next. But for me, the game was over when my mother called me to come inside.

My mother did not like the game and decided I could not play it. She said it was a game of war, and the newspapers were full of the war in Europe, and she was worried. If our country also went to war, she had young brothers and friends who would be called into the army. On December 7, 1941, our worst fears came true. The Japanese had bombed Pearl Harbor. President Franklin D. Roosevelt delivered the news on the radio. We were at war.

Many changes began to occur. With our men being drafted and war plants being set up, my father decided to go from our home in Pennsylvania to New York State where his cousins lived and find a job there. He had an injury to one of his eyes and would not be called into the service. It was also his chance to leave the Pennsylvania coal mining job for work in a war plant.

We would be leaving our beloved home that had once belonged to my paternal grandfather, and we were sad indeed. We had a lovely yard with fruit trees and many flowers.

A neighbor wanted very much to rent our home while we were gone. While we were contemplating the move, my mother discovered another lump. She decided to wait to visit a doctor until after we arrived at our new location. When my father began working at a plant and found an apartment, he sent for us. We had to leave many things behind in our attic. To me, they were prized possessions: my grandfather's clarinet, many old albums, and my prized glow-worm costume. My grandfather and his brothers had a band years ago and played at weddings and dances. I was told he met my grandmother at a dance. When this lovely blonde walked in, my grandfather gave his instrument to his brother and went to dance with the girl from Chicago. She married him and never went back home. I never knew my grandmother, as she died before I was born, but I loved my step-grandmother very much.

Little did I know that we would never again see the things we left in the attic. Years later, when my father sold our house, he never retrieved the items left there.

Chapter 5

Arriving at our new location, my mother and I were disappointed. We found the apartment to be very small with no yard. Our family home had been old but spacious. Now, looking out of the windows, we saw only traffic; no children playing games and having fun. I, also being shy, had a new school to contend with.

As soon as we were settled, my parents began inquiring about doctors in the area. After a visit to one who had been recommended, my mother came home with the news of another operation. We had just arrived, and now she would not be home with us.

She spent a week in the hospital, as they had found two lumps that needed to be removed. When she finally returned home, she appeared thin and pale. I noticed her skin had taken on a yellow tinge. It took a while before she began gaining some weight and getting her energy back.

We were still trying to become accustomed to our new location when we began having air raid practices. When the sirens sounded, all lights in the house had to be off. Streetlights went off too. The air raid wardens were walking the streets, making sure we were all in compliance. They looked very official with their hard hats and nightsticks. We listened for aircraft above us, which could mean this was real and enemy planes had arrived. When the sirens sounded all clear, we were relieved. The streetlights came back on, and everything seemed normal again.

We also had food stamps; things like meat and butter were in short supply. We had a pound of white substance and a small yellow ball, which I would work together until it turned yellow. Now you had to think of it as butter. My father said he had to use his imagination.

We were urged to grow victory gardens. If you had no yard, you hoped someone would share vegetables with you, as they were asked to do.

When banners began appearing in windows, we took notice. They had stars on them. A blue one, as I remember, told of a son in the service. A purple star meant an injured soldier, and the saddest one of all, a gold star was for a serviceman who had given his life for his country.

When our neighbor lost both of her sons, she was inconsolable. How young they had been, handsome and so full of life, and now they would never come home again. It was indeed a time of great sorrow.

Newspapers showed pictures of what was happening in Europe: starving people, children with swollen bellies from lack of food. People did what they could for the war effort. Women went into war plants, hoping to help end this terrible nightmare. We sang songs about Rosie the Riveter. Rosie was dressed in coveralls with a bandanna on her head as she worked diligently on aircraft.

People bought war bonds. We schoolchildren went door to door collecting aluminum cans. Some buildings had a picture of a man with a finger to his lips. It meant *say nothing; the enemy may be listening. Do not tell the enemy where our men are being sent.*

When I received a letter from my uncle in the service, it was a small note with holes in it. That meant things were cut out. If families could come up with a code, then they may know a little more of what was happening to their men.

We had a diversion with some movies. We liked musicals, but the war movies frightened us. What was going to happen? Could the enemies possibly win and come over to take our country from us?

Chapter 6

We had not been to see our relatives for about a year. When we did go, we traveled by train to Pennsylvania. Gas rationing was enforced. When we arrived, my maternal grandmother was baking bread. The aroma filled the house. I loved to watch her pound down that huge mass, put it in a warm place to rise, and then pound it down again before it was ready to place in bread pans in the oven. Grandpa would bring in tomatoes and lettuce from his garden. Never since have I tasted such rich, red, delicious tomatoes. Sandwiches of lettuce and tomatoes on that delicious bread were heavenly. A plate of homemade soup went with it.

We went to see old friends near our house that was being rented; it was very nostalgic. Little did we know at the time that we would never live in our family home again. Things would take a turn that would change my life as I knew it.

We were doing our best to adjust to our new location and small apartment. My mother's sister and her brother, along with their families, also moved to our location and found jobs in war plants. This brought great joy to my mother. She was holding up well, and things were going much better for us, so I felt the worst was over and my mother would be well again. Her energy had returned, and I was happy to see her full of life again.

We had two churches near us, with another down on the corner, making it three. On Sundays, I would watch the people coming out all smiles as the church bells rang. I wondered if we were missing something, but my parents never seemed to notice. Nothing was ever said about religion. As for me, I did think about it. I felt it might be a nice thing to do. I saw no more rosary beads after my Bobka had died, and the church services on the dairy farm were only a dream now.

Chapter 7

oes God really exist? How do we know? How can anyone know? As my mother bid me good night and I snuggled in my bed, this question loomed in my mind. Maybe he is just a myth. The war was causing such pain and suffering; would God just ignore it? Where is he? Maybe nowhere. Is there a way to contact heaven? I'm only eleven; how could I accomplish a feat such as this? My desire to find an answer overcame my fear. Maybe this great being, if he does exist, might be quite friendly. It wouldn't hurt to try to communicate with heaven. *Now,* I thought, *how high up can heaven be? I imagine it must be far, far away.* Closing my eyes and reaching my mind up as far as I could possibly reach, I prayed. "Dear God, can you hear me?"

My mother was busy with a large stack of ironing, and she ironed everything: hankies, dresses; the most difficult to me seemed to be those starched white shirts my father sometimes wore.

I continued with my silent prayer, asking God if he really existed, would he do me a very big favor: to have my busy mother come into my room. I knew she would have no reason to come in, and if she did as I prayed she would, then it would be God who sent her, wouldn't it?

The kitchen in the small apartment was near the bedroom, and I could hear the iron pressing the clothes as my mother worked. Suddenly I heard my mother put down the iron. Lo and behold, she was coming toward the bedroom. She had left the bedroom door open, so the light filtered in. As she entered, she stood awhile and looked around. I asked what it was she was looking for. Shrugging her shoulders, she answered that she did not know. She seemed very bewildered, and I felt a little frightened. As she walked back to finish her ironing, I lay there a bit awestruck. *Can this be? Would a very important "God" really answer a child's prayer?* I came to the conclusion that is the only reason my mother would come into my room, only if God had sent her. A love welled up in my heart. What a kind and caring God he must be! I desired to know all about him and how he works in the world. This was my quest. I would never stop seeking him. But being a very private person, I would never discuss this experience with anyone. I was not encouraged by my parents to speak my mind; hadn't they always reminded me that children should be seen and not heard?

Chapter 8

I was now attending the new school. Being shy, I hoped someone would pick me as a friend. A very nice little girl invited me to come to her house. This made me happy; now I had a friend to walk to school with. This became a lifelong friendship. Soon we had a little group of friends, and I felt happier than I had since moving away from my previous home.

My mother's health became a greater concern. More tumors began to develop, and the doctor, not knowing what other course to take, recommended a clinic in Buffalo, New York. At the clinic, they were trying radiation treatments. It was a new procedure at the time, and they were having some success.

After a few weeks of discussion, my parents decided to go; what other course was there? We contacted some friends who had recently moved from our old area to Buffalo. They welcomed us and asked us to stay a few days with them.

It turned into a small vacation for us as we visited Niagara Falls and were stunned by its magnitude. Our friends showed us many sights to take our minds off the reason we were there. They also had a girl my age, and I was delighted to see her again.

Finally, it was time for my mother to enter the clinic. I was overwhelmed with sadness. I knew we would be leaving her there and going home without her. Not knowing how long she would be there was very disturbing. It was very lonely without her, and when we returned to Buffalo to bring her home again, we had hoped for a better outcome. She looked thin and pale; the treatments, rather than helping, had taken a toll on her health. The treatments had stopped the growth of the tumors but had not removed them, and she had many. They called it Hodgkin's disease; more is known about it now than at that time.

We had hoped for a cure, but it never came. She had some good days, but eventually only medication was given to her for the pain. She began to take to her bed more and more. There came a day when she did not get out of bed and lapsed into a coma. My prayers for my mother seemed to be going nowhere, and I lost my faith that God existed.

Relatives took turns coming to aid us at this time. Our apartment was small and did not accommodate many.

Chapter 9

*B*ecause we had relatives staying with us, I slept on two living room chairs put together to form a bed.

One night while I was asleep, a very vivid dream came to me. In the dream, I arose from my bed and went in to see my mother, but she was not in her bed. I could hear her calling to me, but I could not find her. I looked around in wonder; she was nowhere to be seen. Then I sensed her calling to me from a closet that extended far under the stairs. It seemed very strange to me that she would be in there. I had to push aside all the clothes that hung there before I found her. She was huddled and frightened as she looked out at me. Her eyes were large as she begged me not to let "them" get her. All I could say was, "Who, Mommy, who?" Suddenly something "clicked" in my mind, and the scene changed.

I saw my uncle Larry standing in the bedroom. My mother was now smiling as she came out of the closet. They had reached out to greet each other as I stood aside and watched. They seemed very happy to see each other. I found it strange that my mother was now in a dress and not her bedclothes. And Larry, why was he in a suit? He never wore suits. The only time I saw him in a suit was at his funeral.

Larry was my mother's beloved brother. He had died more than a year before that night. It had been a very tragic time for the family. *How could he be here? What is the meaning of all this?* I wondered.

I thought back to the day we had received the telegram and how my mother had screamed as she read it. Now Larry was here.

He had died in a coal mine explosion. His wife and children were in the next room; they had come to help us as my mother declined in health.

In my dream, as I watched them in wonder, my mother looked toward me. She asked Larry if I could also come with them. How sad I was to hear the answer he gave: "No." My heart was broken, and I would have given anything to go with them, no matter where it would be. *Why could I not go?* I wondered.

Suddenly something woke me from my dream. I was still in my chair-bed, and I heard crying. I ran to my mother's room. My father was telling the relatives how, as he sat by her bed, she awoke from her coma. He said she looked around the room with fear in her eyes. She said nothing but took her last breath and was gone. My beautiful mother was only thirty-two years old. How could I live without her?

Though my dream was still clear in my mind, I told no one. I hardly knew what I had experienced; how could I explain it? I was not close enough to my father to tell him. I just kept it close to my heart. I sat and cried as the family discussed what they would do next.

I sat alone and watched two men arrive and carry out the body of my mother. It was devastating.

We had the funeral in our living room. There was no church service, but the minister who lived next door to us came to the gravesite to say a few words. It was a sad, cold, snowy March day, and to me it felt like the end of the world. You wonder how you can go on.

Anyone who has lost a loved one understands—living with a heavy heart is hard to do, but you go on, one day at a time.

After a few days at home, I was encouraged to go back to school. I was not aware that I had developed a series of tics until I heard some classmates discussing the funny faces I kept making in class.

Because we lived in a small apartment with only one bedroom, I now slept on a couch next to the kitchen coal stove. My father was no longer working nights and needed the bedroom.

I pondered one day, *Where has my mother gone? What happens to us? Where do we go?* I knew we went somewhere, but where? When I finally slept, a vivid dream came to me. I saw my mother, and she was smiling and seemed to be happy and healthy. I asked if she was better now. She replied that she was fine. I asked if she was cured of the cancer. "Yes," she answered, "and don't you worry." It seemed someone was waiting for her and she had to leave.

When I awoke in the morning, I expected to see her. I looked around, feeling very relieved, but when it came to me that it was a dream that had seemed so real, I was distraught. She was not here; I was all alone. Oh, how I missed her.

That day, I received a letter from my father's sister. She was working in New York City as a cook for a wealthy couple. They were taking a trip to Europe and had suggested that I come visit while they were gone. I took the train to New

York. How nice it was to sleep in a beautiful bedroom and go to Broadway shows!

She was the aunt who always helped. She bought me much-needed school clothes.

I remembered in the past when my badly infected tonsils were affecting my health that she had paid the bill for the operation.

My mother was saving money for the surgery and keeping it in the cookie jar. One day when she checked to count her money, the jar was empty. Oddly, my father had come home with a new radio in his car. When a fight ensued between my parents, I was sent outside to wait it out.

Immediately my aunt arrived, and seeing how terrible I looked, she took me to the doctor. He felt I may be coming down with St. Vitus Dance, a disease caused by the infection. My aunt at once had me placed in the hospital for the operation. She had saved me, and she even paid the bill of $800.

Chapter 10

*O*n September 2, 1945, we heard the news. As a friend and I were taking a walk, we heard church bells ringing. Some boys yelled over to us, "The war has ended!" People in cars honked their horns and waved. What we all had been waiting for had finally happened. Peace again! The war, after four years, had finally come to an end. Our boys would be coming home again.

After a while, homes began being built, in clusters. Small, colorful homes, tiny, with three bedrooms, one bathroom, a kitchen, and a living room. Our servicemen, home again, wanted nothing more than to marry their sweethearts and start a family. Greed was not in our vocabulary; world peace was, and we felt now it had finally come. We were happy with whatever we had.

When we went to school—we were in high school now—teachers had an assignment for us. It was time to become acquainted with and learn from children in other countries. My teacher handed out the names and addresses; the one I received had the name of a boy in Russia. His name was Rudolph. It was fun to receive his letters and learn about life in Russia. We wrote for quite a while and then stopped for some reason.

We also were given an assignment to write an essay. We were told the winning essay would appear on the editorial page in our daily newspaper. The topic was to be the hunger in Europe. I began my article with "Somewhere in Europe, a child is crying." It told of hunger and not toys the child was crying about, and it encouraged people to give as much as they could for this effort to buy the necessities for these war-torn countries.

I was surprised when I opened the newspaper and saw my article on the editorial page.

Chapter 11

For some reason unknown to me, startling dreams came to me at night. I would dream of a terrible train accident. In a few days, the accident appeared in the newspaper, just as I saw it in my dream. The train accident happened in an area of Pennsylvania not far from where we had previously lived.

In another dream, a small plane fell from the sky onto the roof of a house. Two men got out of the plane, waved, and smiled in my direction. When the accident appeared in the newspaper, the two men had not lived but had died in the crash.

Another night, while falling asleep, I experienced a feeling of ascending to the ceiling. I was shocked and called out, "Where am I going?" By saying this, I stopped and looked down. There, fast asleep on the bed, was my body. *Could I be dead?* I thought. But looking more closely, I could see I was asleep. There seemed to be two of me.

Many years went by before I read some books explaining astral projection or out-of-body experience. It was only then that I realized what had happened to me.

While in high school, my best friend began pointing out the new foreign students who were appearing in our classes. She was taken with an Italian-looking one. I went along with her; I was always a follower. He wore a ruby-red satin shirt, and it went well with his slick, black hair. When we walked home with him, we found he was an artist. That fascinated us even more. We went out of our way to walk him home. We did not live in that direction, not anywhere near where his home was, but we did not let him know that.

On the way, we would stop so that he could draw for us pictures of war scenes and try to explain them to us in his halting English. We did this for most of the spring semester. We hoped to make him feel welcome in his new country. His father walked by one day, carrying his violin. We were impressed that his father was an accomplished violinist.

We found out that our year of making him feel welcome worked very well. He learned to sing in English, well enough to be in our school program, a talent show. He sang so many songs that the stage crew had to forcibly drag him from the stage. Good for him!

Next we turned our attention to two boys from Persia, the country they now call Iran. Mohammed was quite swarthy-looking. He told us the story of five Persian rugs his parents had sent with him; he could sell them, and the money would help with his expenses in this country. Arriving in New York City, he met a very beautiful Persian woman. He showed us a picture, and she was indeed very lovely. One sad day, the woman disappeared, and his five Persian rugs went with her. He could never forget it, and many times he counted out on his fingers those five beautiful Persian rugs and how great a loss it had been for him.

My best friend and I were very close, as she had also lost her mother; we had our sadness to share with one another. She spent a great deal of time with me at our apartment, as many nights my father was not at home. He, being still in his thirties, was very interested in parties and dating. My friend had a grand sense of humor, and I learned to laugh. We found laughter to be the best medicine, and it helped us both to heal.

After graduation, we looked for employment. She found something rather quickly with an insurance company. It took me a little longer before I found a temporary position with a publishing company. They needed people to help during the busy season, and it would give me some needed experience. They published schoolbooks. When that ended, I went to work for a magazine company. It only lasted one year because the manager had done something illegal, and people came from New York City and closed our branch. We were very disappointed. Next I worked for opticians, loan companies, and ended with a fine paper distributor. I stayed at this company for eight years.

Chapter 12

When my father remarried, he moved into a house with his new wife and some relatives she had living with her. I began apartment hunting with a friend. Our salaries were not large, but we found a place that would do for a time. On weekends, we attended dances in the area and made new friends. We made our money last by eating light.

Dreams began coming to me at night, but I never discussed any of them with friends. I began seeing life as a learning experience. When a voice would explain to me what seemed to be another lifetime and a problem I was now having, I understood this to be a chance to undo a wrong I had done in a past life.

Many years ago, when I was in school, a friend asked if I ever wondered where we were before this lifetime. I felt we were nowhere, that this was our first one. Now I began to think differently.

After a while, my friends began to meet "the one" and weddings took place. I was always the bridesmaid, never the bride. That was much to my liking, as I was in no hurry.

When my friends began to bring adorable babies into the world, I thought, *Well, maybe someday.*

With other jobs, my salary began to increase, and sometimes I had an apartment to myself.

A Catholic friend asked me to make a novena with her. She had a problem. It seems the man she wanted to marry had been married before and had a child. The Catholic Church would not sanction the marriage. A novena, in the Catholic Church, is a beautiful service with incense and music; you must attend once a week for five weeks or so. Then the holy Virgin Mary would give you an answer to your prayer. We had only attended three times when the young man died at her house. He was only twenty-three. The doctor called it a cerebral hemorrhage. I remembered that many times he had suffered headaches. With the devastation of my friend, I worried, had we killed him with our novena? I prayed over this, and the answer came in a dream: he would have died after they had married. She did marry years later, and in the church, as she had wanted to.

Chapter 13

I married at age twenty-eight. I was hoping for a baby, but it did not happen for three years. I decided to make a novena, because at the time, I was also Catholic. Along came a beautiful baby boy, and I was certain novenas do answer prayers.

Many years ago, I had seen pictures of Paris, France. It seemed to be a very beautiful city, with much to see. I longed to visit Paris but had little hope of going there. One day, my husband came home with an offer from his company to spend two years on assignment in Paris. I was amazed at the offer, and after careful consideration, we decided to go. We sailed for France on the S.S. *United States* in April 1963. Our son was only ten weeks old, but he loved the trip and smiled a lot. His mother did not do as well and was seasick for five days.

When we arrived in Paris, we found a beautiful old French house to rent, ten miles outside of Paris in Le Vesinet. It was large, three stories high, with a beautiful garden full of roses. Bees sometimes entered because the windows were large with no screens. The French people loved living with the outdoors. We did have shutters that we closed at night.

Traveling in Europe was exciting. The countries are not very far apart; it was akin to traveling state to state back home. I found the changes of language, customs, and foods very interesting. The French people love to relax and talk over dinner. The Germans eat, sing, and dance to fast-paced bands. In Spain, they did the tango, beautifully at that.

On January 1, 1965, we welcomed another beautiful baby boy, born in the Paris American Hospital. Now our first son would have a playmate. Instead of staying for the designated two years, we stayed four.

Traveling with two babies was a challenge. But travel we did! We would not leave them behind with a nanny. We would need to turn the back seat of our Peugeot into a sort of playpen. Seat belts were unheard of back then. My husband used a wooden platform and covered it with thick foam. Our boys loved it as long as they had toys to play with. When they were sleepy, it made a perfect bed.

Having the US military facilities that we could use made stopping at the post exchanges (PXs) very handy. My husband's company was attached to a defense communication project with the military.

On one of our trips to Italy, we encountered a huge rainstorm. It was the year Florence flooded, destroying many famous paintings. We were on a road that was suddenly being washed away. It was frightening. A group of Italian men came upon the scene and helped push all the stranded cars along and out of the flooded road. We were very grateful; it was becoming dark, and we needed to get our babies to the hotel. In the city, all lights were out. By luck or the help of

God, our headlights hit upon a billboard giving directions to the hotel we were looking for.

It was very dark, but we found the front door of the hotel and entered. Luckily, the concierge met us and held a large candle. Speaking in Italian, she cooed over our babies and led us up a winding staircase. She lit some candles in our room and departed. We wondered what the next morning would bring, but we were awakened by the sun streaming into our windows.

Our trip turned out to be very enjoyable; so much history in that wonderful country. We visited Rome, St. Peter's, Venice, Sorrento, the isle of Capri, Pisa, Pompeii—not all in one trip, of course, but in the three trips we made there. We also enjoyed Spain, the Netherlands, Denmark, Switzerland, Austria, Monaco, and Great Britain on future trips.

When we made a trip to Germany, I was very excited about visiting some old castles, and we had an amazing experience. We went to see some beautiful castles in Bavaria. They had been built in 1869 by the king of Bavaria. We saw three of the most beautiful and were fascinated. When we arrived at the one called Neuschwanstein, which is in the northern region, we had a long hill to climb. It was quite a sight to behold. In fact, Cinderella's castle at Disney World is inspired by Neuschwanstein Castle.

As we were climbing the hill, I had a distinct feeling of having been on this path before. But this was impossible, as we had never before been to Germany. As we walked and took in the beautiful scenery, a dream came back to me, a dream I remembered from long ago when I was sixteen. In the dream, I was running down a hill very much like this one, and as I looked back, I saw a lonely man standing high up on the hill, with a beautiful castle in the background. He wore a blue uniform that I did not recognize. I noticed his head full of thick black curls. He seemed very, very sad. In the dream, I remembered my fear kept me from going back to him. Then I had heard a voice say, "You ran away from love, and you will suffer because of this." When I awoke with a start, the dream was still very clear in my mind, and I never forgot it. I remembered the dream as we walked that hill; some problems in this lifetime came back to haunt me.

After viewing the castle, we stopped at the gift shop, and I felt compelled to buy a book about King Ludwig II. He had only spent a few months living in the castle, when he was taken by guards to Berg Castle and kept prisoner there. After returning from our trips, I went to the military base's bookstore. I hoped to find some books on psychic phenomena. I needed some help figuring out what was happening to me. I found a book called *There Is a River,* the story of Edgar Cayce. I read it cover to cover. I found they had an organization called the Association for Research and Enlightenment, and I certainly needed to be enlightened, as I was in the dark.

I joined in 1965, and I received their newspaper and list of books to order. I felt I had found a home with like-minded people. I ordered several books, including one on dreams. I found this to be of much help. We were encouraged to keep a journal of our dreams. It stated that God speaks to us through our dreams. I also learned to meditate. For spiritual growth, this seemed to be the most helpful practice one can do.

We were told to ask a question before sleep and keep our journal and a pen handy to jot down the answer we received as soon as we awoke and remembered a dream. Dreams have a way of fading from our minds as the day goes on, although a few important dreams will stay with us for a very long time.

Our life in Paris proved to be very interesting. In the sixties they were cleaning the buildings of soot that had accumulated over many years. The Parisians were not happy with the cleaning; they felt the old, dark look gave the city its character. When they saw what lay under the soot of the opera house, they were amazed and began to change their minds. The colors were cream, pale green, and soft pink—a wonderful sight of beauty.

Outdoor markets were close to our house. You carried your own basket to pick out wonderful, fresh vegetables. The French people shopped for them on a daily basis, as refrigerators were tiny. We also purchased delicious loaves of French bread daily. We made the mistake of asking for the bread to be put in a wrapper. "No, no," we were told, "no wrapper. That would take away from the nice, crisp crust." Many times the French children were sent to buy bread. It was either tied on the back of their bicycle or they carried several loaves in their arms with a smile on their faces. You could tell how large the family was by the number of loaves they carried.

Chapter 14

*J*n 1967, we sailed away from France, arriving in New York City. Our next assignment was to be in Los Angeles, California. After visiting relatives, we headed west. The drive was very picturesque, and we stopped along the way at many interesting spots, including the Grand Canyon and Painted Forest.

When we arrived in Los Angeles, we rented an apartment and hoped to locate a house very soon. After many unsuccessful ventures, we saw an ad in the newspaper about some houses being built in a place called Simi Valley. We drove to the San Fernando Valley and found the pass that would take us to the valley we were looking for. The pass was very rugged and a perfect picture of the Old West, with large boulders along the way. We loved it, and the news reported that a new highway would be built in the future. When we reached the valley, we found the orange groves giving off a wonderful aroma, and the new homes were lovely and at a reasonable price. It did not take us long to purchase one we liked.

When we finally moved in, the rains came. The rains were very heavy and unusual for California's dry climate. Our side entrance flooded quite quickly, and we knew we had to build this up higher as soon as the rains subsided. The higher patio entrance we put in went well with the house design, which was adobe.

So now we felt very settled in—until the fires came. Since we had mountains on both sides of our small valley, it did not take the fire long to jump over the highway to the other mountain. Now we were hemmed in. The firefighters called on bullhorns to be ready to evacuate. We packed what we could and had it waiting by the front door. Luckily, the great California firefighters put the fires out, and we were saved. We settled in to enjoy the beautiful area and mild climate. That is until the earthquakes arrived. More about that later.

When we took trips out of our valley, we of course had to venture over the pass, which was called Santa Susana Pass. I noticed a place called Spahn Ranch, which was an old Western movie set where they offered pony rides. How nice for our children to ride in a real Hollywood movie set. *We must do this one day,* I thought! One bright, sunny day, we had time, and I suggested it might be a good day for a pony ride.

After stopping and preparing to go in, I noticed three people, one man with long hair and a beard, two women in long dresses, beads and very long hair also. The man appeared very short and was looking up at another man who was on a horse. In those days, we referred to them as hippies. I felt uneasy, and when an inner voice spoke within me and I heard "Do not go in there," I asked my husband to please drive on. Never would we enter Spahn Ranch again.

One day, when my husband worked very late, as he sometimes needed to do, I was alone with the children. By this time, we had a beautiful daughter, born in 1969. I noticed an old van with ragged curtains in its windows parked between our house and the neighbor's. *Who could that be?* I wondered, as I had never seen a van like that in our neighborhood before.

I felt very uneasy, as I heard voices coming from near our side entrance. It seemed to be a discussion on what they planned to do. One voice said, "No," and the other answered, "But Charlie said to!" I froze for a moment, wondering what was going on. It was very late and strange that anyone would be out. What would I do if they came to my door? But after a while, I heard nothing. When I looked out our window, the van was still there.

The next morning, my neighbor rang my doorbell to tell me her story. The van had stayed there all night, but in the morning, it was gone. Some people had been at her door, asking to use her phone. It was late, and she refused. They had loosened her doorknob by turning it over and over again. She had seen one man and two women dressed as hippies. Why had she not called the police? A few months later, she sold her house and moved away.

Not too long afterward, a murder occurred in Beverly Hills on Cielo Drive. It was Saturday, August 9, 1969 when the newspapers reported the killing of five people, one being the movie star Sharon Tate.

When they finally arrested the Charles Manson family, I recognized Charles Manson as the man I had seen at the Spahn Ranch that day. The man on the horse looked like the man they called "Shorty." He ran the ranch and had disappeared. I don't think they ever found him.

Later, the stories of the Manson family driving around in an old van gave me chills, remembering the van parked near my house. It was such a horrendous crime that even seasoned investigators and detectives were appalled at the sight. Eventually the house on Cielo Drive was torn down by the new owners.

One day, new neighbors moved into the house next door to mine. The neighbor was a writer and had tickets to the Academy Awards. They invited us to attend with them! The awards were held at the beautiful Dorothy Chandler Pavilion. This was an exciting experience for us. I was thrilled to walk the red carpet and see the glamorous stars that I had only seen on the big screen. The year was 1969, and the movie *Patton* won for Best Picture. I had to pinch myself to realize that I was really there.

Chapter 15

While in California, I was invited to join an Edgar Cayce study group. It involved a book called *A Search for God* and daily meditation. We had seven members, and we met once a week. We shared our dreams and meditated together. It was a very enlightening experience and did much for my dream experiences; the dreams became clearer and had deeper meaning. Dreams help us to see what may happen in the future, when we look back at what we had written and see the meaning of a dream.

One dream I had was very clear and began with a ringing of the doorbell. When I opened the door, my aunt stood there, my father's sister. She told me my father had died. I noticed my mother's brother in-law standing behind my aunt. That was the end of the dream. It took six months to understand the meaning. In six months, my aunt called me; the relative standing with her in the dream had called her. My father had died.

Can our lives be preordained? Do we somehow have a way of seeing into the future? My father had been suffering for many years due to black lung disease, the result of his long years of working in the coal mines.

I continued searching and reading any books I could find on the subject. One day, I came across a book called *Nothing So Strange* by the medium Arthur Ford. He wrote about the connection we have of one mind to another. Being curious, one night I tried to talk to my son mentally. I could hear him from my bed as he seemed to be having a nightmare. Mentally I encouraged him not to be afraid but instead to see a garden full of beautiful roses.

At breakfast the next morning, my son began to tell me of a frightening dream he'd had. After explaining what had frightened him, he talked about walking out into a garden. He said first he had a bad dream, and then suddenly he was in a garden full of the most beautiful roses he had ever seen. I was shocked; I did not feel that this could really happen. Now I wondered how true this could be.

After trying one more night, I was convinced. When he was asleep, I mentally communicated to him to walk into our back yard and see many beautifully colored birds. The next morning, he explained what he had dreamed, about many colorful birds in our back yard.

We are really of one mind if we are spiritually connected to someone. Jesus had prayed that we may all be of one mind, as he was with his Father. Read John 17:20.

I kept on praying and seeking.

I had an experience with a woman in our meditation study group. She seemed antagonistic toward me, which I could not understand, as I had never met her before. A dream I had one night brought me an understanding of why this was occurring. In the dream, I was told of a past lifetime in which this woman had wanted a certain man very badly, but he had married me, and she had never gotten over it. This holding on to past grievances was affecting her life now. In this lifetime, her first husband had died, and now her second husband had suddenly left her. I understood this to mean you should let things go if you don't want to carry baggage with you to future lives. I wondered whether I needed to explain my dream to her, but she suddenly left our group, and I never saw her again.

Chapter 16

*O*ne day on California television, there appeared a faith healer named Kathryn Kuhlman. She said, "I believe in miracles because I believe in God." She spoke very slowly, due to a stutter she had as a child. To my astonishment and joy, she would be appearing at the Shrine Auditorium in Los Angeles. A friend and I found that a bus would be taking a group of people from our area to the service.

When we arrived, it seemed because of the crowd, my friend and I would not be able to enter. We sat on the outside steps, and after a while, a man opened the door and asked us to come in. We were at the service for six hours, listening to heavenly music and watching beautiful Kathryn invite people to the stage if they had been healed. On the stage with her were people of many faiths: nuns, ministers, priests, doctors, and more. I could feel the Holy Spirit in that place. Kathryn never touched a person.

She said, in her slow, deep voice, "The glory belongs to God alone!" On her television program, people appeared who had been healed in her services. They must have an affidavit proving a healing that even the doctors could not understand. The healing of children especially touched my heart. One mother said she screamed to God when she found her beautiful three-year-old daughter had leukemia. Her daughter had a complete healing at the services.

We lost Kathryn Kuhlman when she passed from this life on February 20, 1976. While she was with us, people gained much.

As my dreams continued, I awoke one morning to tell my husband that my maternal grandmother would be passing on. She had appeared in my dream to say good-bye. My deceased grandfather was with her, and luggage was in the background. They looked happy and full of color, even younger than their years. They had been in their eighties! Death is not a terrible thing as some imagine it to be, but a happy time when a life well lived has come to an end.

A very surprising dream occurred to me one night. I awoke one morning with the feeling that I could write the name I was called in a past lifetime. I felt I could use the same handwriting I had used then. This lifetime had happened a long time ago, when I lived along the Rhine River in Germany. The shock to me was that I had been male. I had a picture in my mind of a tall, blond male. I remembered he held an important part in the family, far exceeding any of the females. I had felt very important then, and it was a family of good means. I also remember my name was Wilhelm.

A voice in the dream was trying to convey to me my last name, but all I could get was that it began with the letter H. It seemed to be an important part of the dream, because then a conveyor belt began to run, and on the belt were dolls. My stuttering and sputtering ended up with me yelling out "Hummel!" and I woke up. I never did find out if a Wilhelm Hummel was ever connected with the famous Hummel figurines. The figurines are named for Sister Maria Innocentia Hummel, whose artwork of children inspired the figurines.

Chapter 17

*A*fter spending five years in California, we again transferred. But before we left California, something happened in the dream state: I awoke one morning with the word "Silmar" on my lips. I spoke the word in a low, mysterious voice, and it made me uneasy.

Several days later, something woke me up at about six a.m. The whole room was shaking. Closet doors were banging, and things on the dresser were jumping about. It was an earthquake. Calling for my six- and eight-year-old boys to join me, I ran to my two-year-old daughter's room. She was standing up in her crib. My husband had worked that night, so we were alone. Trying to reach her, I was thrown back several times. I had heard the best place to be in an earthquake was under a doorframe. I told my eight-year-old to kneel under the doorframe, as we could barely stand up.

My six-year-old did not come, but had stayed in bed. I was unable to reach my daughter, so I began to pray for God's help to reach her. Suddenly, all the shaking stopped, but as soon as I had her, the rumbling started just as bad as it had been. We were unable to move and stayed under the doorframe saying the Lord's Prayer. One of the quakes had gone side to side and the next one up and down. The epicenter was, as I had dreamed, in a place called Silmar. Sixty-nine people had died.

When we transferred, it was to Colorado. The climate was nice and the mountains beautiful. I did miss California but not the many aftershocks we always had to endure.

In Colorado, we had conferences in our beautiful Rocky Mountains. Hugh Lynn Cayce came and brought his lovely wife, Sally. He had stories about growing up as the son of Edgar Cayce. He was very wise and spiritual, and we learned much from him. It was a pleasure for me to meet him.

Chapter 18

We acquired a puppy we named Lady. She was a shaggy mutt, but she had a dignified name. We all loved her, and she became one of our children. She was calm and well-behaved; only one thing bothered her: any popping sounds. In the car one day, the children popped bubble gum, and Lady wanted out of the car. She seemed terrified, and we could not understand her problem.

One day, as I sat alone petting Lady, the inner voice spoke to me. "This is the same dog you had once before." The only other dog I had as a child was Mickey. He was a shaggy dog also. The story of Mickey came back to haunt me. For no reason, Mickey was taken out in a car and shot. The person had a new rifle, but the shot was not clean, and a bleeding Mickey came back home and was taken out again to finish the job. How many tears can be shed? Mine come again as I tell this story.

When I was still single I had a yellow parakeet I called Petey. He learned to talk, as he was very smart. He loved to be out of his cage. One Saturday, he was up early, so I took him to bed with me, and he had a chance to fly around the apartment. After I awoke, Petey would be asleep until I woke up, and he was under the blanket.

He made me realize how wonderful birds are. Many years after Petey, we found a bird's nest held in place by our downspout. We had been away and did not return until spring. The nest was close to our sun room window, and when the bird saw us, she became nervous. I stayed far away from the window until she grew accustomed to us.

One day, as I was weeding my garden, I noticed the mother bird on the fence watching me. By luck, I happened to find a worm, so I threw it toward her and motioned for her to take it to her nest. I went inside to watch from the window, and I saw she found the worm and took it to her nest. I noticed she pushed aside two birds to get to the other underneath. They were my bird family, and I loved them.

One morning, I was informed by my husband that my birds had flown; the nest was empty. I was very sorry I did not see them fly. I took one last look at the nest and went to get my morning coffee. An urge came over me to go back to the sun room, so I took my coffee to have it there. To my surprise, I saw the mother bird and her three babies. When she saw me in the window, she came to our patio and brought her babies with her. She had a worm in her mouth and reached over to the smallest bird to feed it the worm. I seemed to hear her say, "Look, I am feeding my smallest bird." She seemed to be thanking me for the help I had given her in feeding her young. We were two mothers enjoying a special moment together. With tears in my eyes and a smile on my lips, I flapped my arms like wings to let her know my joy that they were now flying. They stood for a moment, looking at me, and then flew away. I thought my heart would burst with joy about the kinship we have with all life.

I never cared for snakes until we had a green garden snake living among us. It kept itself hidden, and we only saw it once as a baby. Many years later, when we sold our house, the snake came out to see us go. It was larger now and seemed upset at our leaving.

My daughter also had a snake story. She never knew she had snakes in her yard; the snakes always kept them selves hidden. They sold the house, the moving van came, and the snakes came out—three in all. When the cleaning lady was leaving their house, she later found one of the snakes had crawled into her car through a hole in the floorboard. She was too far away to bring it back, so she had to drop it off in a field. I guess the snake was saying, "*Take me with you. I love you*".

Explaining our story to a friend, she replied "Oh yes, we have a mother snake and her babies; they live under our house. Whenever my husband does yard work, they all come out and watch him work."

Chapter 19

S ome of my dreams made me laugh at times. When I awoke one morning, I said to my husband, "I had such a funny dream last night." In the dream, I had my husband by the arm as I encouraged him with, "Let me help you walk. That's what marriage is all about." I expected him to laugh also at such a silly idea. But his answer was, "You should have seen what happened to me last night." He had worked well past midnight, and on the way home, he ran out of gasoline. With no gas stations in the vicinity, he had to walk home. I guess it was not so funny after all. Maybe I was there in spirit to make sure he arrived home safely.

At times, my dreams were not very pleasant. I recalled one I had several years ago. It seems a person I knew very well had passed on. This person was not very caring of others; in fact, he bordered on being selfish and even somewhat evil. The dream I had was hearing him call to me from a very dark place. When I went toward the dark, I could see several people there in the darkness with him.

It was very dark, and as I entered the darkness I came to realize that I had a "light" with me. When those in the darkness saw the light, they crowded forward, and I head one whisper, "She has the key." I knew then that the "light" was the key.

Years later, as I studied Edgar Cayce, I came upon a reading that stated: Some souls may go into outer darkness after death. It seemed to me because of some evil they had done while on earth. God always will offer a way out. The desire for light will be great and the souls will seek the light of God.

I once heard about a study done by a doctor who had been interested in how the brain works when one is "in love." He felt it would be a good study, as Valentine's Day was approaching. He questioned how the brain reacts when people are madly in love, and he asked for volunteers to assist him, people who claimed to be very much in love. He took pictures of brainwaves and was surprised to find the "reward center" lighting up when they thought about the loved one. He said it was not much different from what lit up while eating a delicious bar of chocolate. Even more surprising to him was that the reward center is quite near the part of the brain that causes mental problems. Okay, I get it, that's what it means when we say we are crazy in love.

There is a way to love that is beyond this planet (Mark 3:31). As Jesus spoke to the people when they told him, his mother and brothers were outside wishing to speak to him. He replied, "Who are my mother and brothers but all those who hear the Word of God and act upon it". Jesus prayed for all believers, that we may be one as he and his father are one (John 17:20).

There is a love beyond the love we experience daily; it is called *agape love*. I once heard a Dutch lady explain it this way: During World War II she had been hiding Jewish people from the Nazis, and because of that, they held her in a concentration camp. One day after she had been freed, she saw the German general coming down the street toward her. He was one of the cruel ones at the camp she and her sister had been in. She had no love for him and did not desire to even look at him. But he was suddenly standing next to her with his hand outstretched. After a short prayer, she took his hand, and a wave of great love overcame her. She knew it was not her love but one that had come from God. She called it *agape love*. One day I experienced this love when a group of people at a meeting were very argumentative. A friend sitting with me became very irritated with the people and stood up to tell them how she felt. Suddenly I felt a great light in the room and was overcome with a great love for everyone in the room. When she sat back down, still sputtering, I whispered to her, "Just love them."

Later that night, I told her what I had experienced, and she asked me, "Is that why you said to love them?" I explained that it was not me but God's love. Weeks later, after we had prayed together, she also had the experience. We agreed that heaven would be filled with this great love radiating from our God.

Chapter 20

A nimals love as we do, even more. Tabby, our cat, was not happy when a stray black cat came to our door. His black-and-white fur looked great, so we called him Tuxedo. She used to slap him in the face, but he never retaliated. After a while, they became great friends. Our dog, Lady, warmed to him immediately, and she became the guardian of both cats.

One day, the neighborhood cat came creeping across our lawn. Tuxedo was enjoying a nap under our pine tree. "Big Gray," as we called him, was a bully and loved a good fight. Lady, asleep at my feet, sensed Big Gray before I did. She was up and out of the door, pursuing the intruder. Lady had been sound asleep and never really saw the cat coming. They have telepathy, I have found.

Tabby and Tuxedo walked across the lawn one day, looking at each other. They were communicating. He would jump up into the air, and then Tabby would do likewise. I was puzzled by it. One windy day, I understood: he was teaching her to jump for birds. When the wind blows, a bird cannot fly well. A bird was on the ground finding a worm when Tux sprang at it. It was such a beautiful robin, but the cat had it before I could do anything. After that, I kept them in on windy days, even though they were displeased with me. They were well-fed cats, I might add, and did not need a bird.

It was a sad day when our beloved Lady dog passed away. Pets become so much a part of the family; we all grieved.

Within a few weeks the children felt another dog would be nice to have. With everyone so busy with school and activities, I was the main dog-waste retriever, and felt I could use a rest. Maybe someday in the future, we could think about getting another dog.

While I was sitting with my coffee one morning, my inner voice spoke to me. I heard, "Remember Sandy?" Ah yes, it all came back to me. My relative had a cute dog many years ago. Her name was Sandy, and how sweet she was!

A sad thing happened one day. Sandy, still very young, had run out into the street and was killed by a car. The young man driving the car was distraught. How sad we all were to lose her. It seemed I was being urged to get ready for the return of Sandy. Well, I did not plan on going out to find Sandy, and I promptly forgot about it. After a few days the memory of Sandy came back to me again. I said to God, "Father, if this is your urging, then you will have to drop her in my lap." I knew this would never happen. Lady had been gone only a few weeks, and I was not about to go out looking for another dog.

I felt I had this all worked out, as dogs do not fall from heaven. Does God have a sense of humor? I think he does. He had other plans.

My son, the one who is a great animal lover, was out taking a walk one day and came upon a lonely, lost puppy.

Before he brought it home, he assured me he had looked everywhere and had knocked on every door, and no one had ever seen this dog. Now what was I to do? Especially since I noticed this pup had a strong resemblance to the one God reminded me of, Sandy.

My children begged and pleaded, promising that they would take care of all the puppy's needs. I would not have to do a thing. (You can imagine how *that* turned out.)

While all this talk was going on, the pup kept looking at me with soulful eyes. We tried to find the dog's owner, but to no avail. She became ours, and we called her Sugar. She looked like brown sugar, and later, while looking over old pictures of Sandy, I was amazed at how much they looked alike. I was glad God did not take me seriously about not wanting another dog. Sugar was so much fun. She was small and loved to sit on our laps. We couldn't imagine life without her. She brought us many days of joy and laughter. She was very playful and would drag an old, small, red bathrobe that we had given her over to us. We called it the "red devil," and it was a great tug-of-war game. When we said, "Where is red devil?" she would run to get it, full of holes as it was, to bring it to us. If she bit me accidentally through one of the holes, she looked very apologetic and moved her head to a better spot with no hole to bite through.

One day, I became sick with heart palpitations and had to spend some time in the hospital. When I came back home after this episode, I began having strange dreams. A figure dressed in gray with a hood covering his face would come down the hall and toward my bed. Knowing him to be evil, I would wake up with a scream. This would wake up my family too. This went on for several nights, and with each dream, the figure would get closer to my bed.

In the last dream, the hooded figure was right over me, and I screamed, "Are you here in the name of Christ?" With that, the figure went up in a cloud of smoke and never returned.

Chapter 21

*M*any years ago, when a friend moved away, we wrote to each other. We had worked at the same place of employment. She wrote to me that she was expecting her first child. After a while, I had a dream, in which she had given birth to a baby girl. When I saw a large number 3 in the dream, I wrote to her, telling her of my dream. She wrote back and said, "I think you must be psychic. I had a baby girl, and she was born three weeks early." We had a laugh over this and wondered why I had this strange ability.

One of my more profound dreams came about one day many years ago, when I was feeling despondent over a problem. In the dream, I stood near a huge oak tree. There was a man in the distance, dressed in a long robe, with sandals on his feet and a lack of hair on his head. He was saying something to three people, and they seemed very interested in him. I began straining to hear what was being said. The man, becoming aware of me, came forward to face me. He said only one sentence: "Have faith, daughter. God has a city prepared for those that are his!" In my heart, I felt I knew him; it was St. Paul.

In the morning, I turned to my Bible. I had not read much about St. Paul. I usually stopped reading after the gospel of Jesus. I only knew that he had experienced a "light" on the road to Damascus. So I began to search; had he ever said anything about a "city," I wondered. I did a lot of reading that day. I read through Ephesians, Colossians, Corinthians, Galatians, but there was nothing about a city. I was about to give up until I got to Hebrews 11:16.

There it was: "What is faith, faith is the substance of things hoped for, the evidence of things not seen." It went on to tell of the men and women who had faith, who struggled and went on, even though in their lifetime they did not receive the promises hoped for, but acknowledged themselves to be strangers and foreigners on this earth. They knew that the earth was not their real home, but that God had a "city" prepared for them.

Life was never easy for Paul. A mob almost killed him, five times he received forty lashes, he was beaten with rods three times, stoned, shipwrecked three times, and imprisoned to name a few, but on he went until in the end, he reached his glory!

Chapter 22

One day, my memory went back to when I was single and had a roommate. When I came in from running some errands, I found my aunt (who was visiting) and my friend having a dispute about religion. It seemed senseless to me, but on and on it went. When we all went to bed, I felt forlorn. I never liked confrontation. I was always one to say nothing.

When I fell asleep, I heard a voice say, "They will die at the same time." I felt this to be unlikely, as the age difference between the two was thirty years. I never gave it a second thought until twenty years later. My aunt passed away at age seventy-nine, in the month of February.

A mutual friend came to visit me. At the time, they had been passing through our area. She asked me if I had heard that my former roommate, Helene, had died. I had not. She had died in February also. I remembered the night I had been given the message. How strange; I had never felt that would really happen.

A few months later, a dream came to me. It began with a knock on my front door. When I opened the door, I heard someone say, "Would you break bread with Helene?" I cried, "Oh, yes, of course!" There stood Helene, and I ushered her in and was very happy to see her.

We went into the kitchen and sat at the counter. I remembered the breaking of bread at the Catholic church, so I looked to see what I had and found crackers, as they reminded me of the host at church. With no wine in sight, we shared tea. As we broke the cracker between us, all sense of any disagreements we had dissolved into the air. It was a wonderful evening, and then she was gone. I know we will meet again.

Chapter 23

*O*ne day, I heard a minister on a radio program talking about the Holy Spirit. He said the Spirit does talk to us and that if we think we hear him tell us to do something, we should obey. He said the more we obey, the more we will hear his voice and the more faith we will have in him. We will see how things work out when we do, and our faith will increase. I found this to be true. He also said even if we are not sure that we are hearing his voice, listen to what we are told and act upon it; we will be surprised at its truth.

After I had listened to that program, I was at the library one day. I wanted a novel, nothing from the religious section, as I felt I needed a little light reading. Well, I felt I heard *"Go to the religious books."* I was not sure I heard correctly, so I tried to ignore the message. When I heard the message come again, I felt I must go. While I stood there wondering what special book was there for me, a woman approached. She really opened up her heart to me. She had many problems in her life, and she revealed private things to me. It was sad, and I felt I had also experienced such things. Looking over the books, I picked out a few, in particular, my favorite,

The Helper, written by Kathryn Marshall, the wife of Peter Marshall, the Scottish minister who had a movie made of his life, *A Man Called Peter.*

After she left and I went back to the novels to find a book for myself, I prayed for the dear woman and was glad I had responded to the message.

One day, a friend in my neighborhood came to me with a question. We had talked many times about dreams and the help they could bring us. She had a friend who had lost a husband during the Vietnam War. He was declared missing in action. My neighbor wondered if I could help in finding what had happened to him. Not promising her any results but saying I would try my best, I knelt that night by my bedside. After asking God for help in this endeavor and placing paper and pen on the bedside to record any dreams that might come, I fell asleep. Very early in the morning, I awoke with a very clear and vivid recall of my dream.

This was the dream: I began flying without any assistance over many green trees; as I looked down it seemed to be a very thick jungle. I was enchanted with the landscape and was actually enjoying the trip. Suddenly I began descending, and seeing a building in the clearing, I went toward it. Finding a door, I entered. A man was standing inside the door, and he bid me enter. He then ushered me into a very large room. Looking around the room, I was amazed to see several solid gold caskets. He asked me if I would like to view the remains, and said if I so desired, he would lift the lids of the caskets.

Knowing I would not recognize the soldiers, as I had never met any of them, I declined. The man very gently suggested to me to encourage people who were suffering the loss of their loved ones in this war to contact each other.

They would be able to comfort each other and know these soldiers were not "missing" anymore, but were now safe and honored (as the gold caskets suggested) and had gone on to their rewards.

I quickly jotted down the dream and that day presented the dream to my neighbor, who was thankful to receive any news of the soldiers. We hoped this would lessen the pain the relatives had been suffering for a very long time.

Chapter 24

*W*e have many churches in our country, and I have visited several of them, always finding something to ponder and embrace in each one. You may not agree with all things coming from the pulpit. I began contemplating the many avenues I had traveled in my search for God, from my early days at the Seventh - day Adventist church I attended with grandparents to my later attendance at the Catholic Church. In my search, I had read many books, finding Edgar Cayce and the Association for Research and Enlightenment (ARE) most uplifting. I read *The Great Religions of the World* and found much in common among them. Arthur Ford, the great psychic of the thirties and forties, had much to offer. I read *Nothing so Strange,* his autobiography, a very fascinating book.

I remembered the wonderful healing services at the Shrine Auditorium in Los Angeles with the beautiful Kathryn Kuhlman. Where had this all led me? What else did I need to do to feel I had accomplished what would fulfill me? I had found meditation to be of great help. It had opened many doors for me, as it had for many people, the door to our higher minds. What book had I missed reading? What church had I failed to enter? Something had kept gnawing at me, suggesting that somehow there was something more. I would let it go, but it kept coming back.

Chapter 25

*O*ne day, I decided to search for God in a different way. It happened at night, after a long meditation and cleansing bath. While on my bed, I began to pray and empty my mind of everything. Things I had heard in church, read in books, been told by others—nothing would be left but an empty mind that I hoped God would fill with his truth. As I closed my eyes and reached my mind as far up to the heavens as I felt it would go, I began my affirmation: "God show me only your truth."

I stayed in silence for what seemed like a long time. Maybe I fell asleep; I do not know. A popping sound in my mind caused me to open my eyes. I was not in bed; I was somewhere else. I felt more wonderful than I had ever felt before. *I was home!* So glorious to finally be home. I had been away for a very long time. There is no peace anywhere on earth like the indescribable feeling of this peace.

It is difficult to explain the feeling I had; it is so overwhelming. Suddenly I realized I was not alone, and although it was very clear and bright, I did not see anyone.

Then I heard a voice; it said something, but I don't remember what it was. I asked him, "How did I arrive here?"

He answered me very kindly. "You found your way through the maze." *How could this be?* I wondered. *Little insignificant me? I'm not an accomplished person. I never did any "big" thing.* I was very perplexed, and then he showed me a person sitting with eyes closed, in sort of a daydream state. It was me; I had never left my heavenly home. It became very clear to me that earth is but our dream; only heaven is real, and we have never left here—not really! It was a surprise and yet very simple.

As I was wondering who the voice could be, I was interrupted by the voice saying, "God wants to see you." Now I was certain a huge mistake had been made. Why would God want to see little me? This sort of thinking did not go on very long, because I was zapped quickly to another place. Now I was in front of a wonderful, pure light, in an oval shape. Even though I did not seem to have a body, I felt that I had fallen to my knees. I was bowing before my God. I mentally said, *Dear God, I am not good enough to be here*, and then I began confessing all my sins, one by one. I felt I had a long way to go before my confession was done. God stopped me with his laugh. God was finding me amusing! His laugh made it very clear to me, and no words could make it any clearer, that God does not see me as sinful. He sees me as he originally created me, and that is perfect; a perfect creation of his making. He loves us all without measure. I would never want to leave him.

Would I be able to stay in this wonderful place? God was reading my thoughts, as I was his. We were not speaking audibly. I heard, *Of course, I want to give you everything!* What could "everything" be, as now I seemed to have everything?

The "angel voice" came to me again: "Are you certain you want to stay?" God had indicated to me that I would be going to a higher place than the place I was now in.

Suddenly the faces of my family came to me, three small children. How could I leave them? I asked whether my family would come with me. The angel's answer was no; for them there would be a body. Oh, how sad for them to not know that I was still alive, in a place of reality, not dead as they would see me. The answer was very clear to me: I must go back and raise my children. The angel acknowledged my need to return to earth.

I was led to a place that would facilitate my return. I became a little frightened at the idea of falling into a dark place. It seemed to me that I would be jumping into a dark lake, and I cannot swim! I began to panic, but I think the kind angel may have given me a shove, for the next thing I knew, I was sailing through a dark maze. I saw the face of a man and knew it to be mankind. Why doesn't everyone know the truth? I felt such sympathy for those who do not. It is all very simple, really. We dream while safe at home.

Suddenly I felt a thud, and I was back in bed. From the ceiling came a white light that entered my forehead. It hurt me profusely. The light entered the area just above my eyes. The nearest gland to the eyes being the pituitary, and a little further up is the pineal gland. Some people say that this is our third eye. We sometimes see the women in India wear a jewel, or a circle of color there.

I decided to get up, but I could not walk. I was unsteady, as if my spiritual body was not completely attached to my physical body. So I stayed in bed, overwhelmed with God's love for us. I felt humble. We have a Father, and he is King of the Universe. (We are not little!) He is waiting for us to return home. We should be willing to make our wills one with his.

Who can give us more, who can love us more than the Great Creator? We need to be as forgiving of others as he is of us.

Later on, as I sat one day and contemplated the experience I'd had, it suddenly came to me that it was the story, as told by Jesus, of the Prodigal Son.

The story told of a son who, after asking for his inheritance, took a journey into a far-off country, where he squandered his money on dissolute living. When he came to his senses, he decided to go back home to his father, and he said, "Father, I have sinned against heaven and you, and I am not worthy to be called your son." But his Father did not view him as a sinner and called for a robe, sandals for his feet, and a jeweled ring for his finger. "For this my beloved son was dead, but is now alive, he was lost and now is found" (Luke 15:12).

While we are still on this planet, we reap what we sow. We must abide by the laws of nature. The wrong eating or drinking will make us sick; steal and you go to jail; wrong someone and you will pay! It may be in this lifetime or the next.

Our Father waits for us to come out of the darkness and into his light. God is love; there is no condemnation in him, but it is in us.

I see it as a puzzle of a large, beautiful picture. If pieces of the puzzle are still missing, the picture is not yet completed. We are the pieces.

Chapter 26

*A*fter having my beautiful experience with God, I wondered if I would ever again be able to reach that place. After all, I had left it willingly. I will leave you dear children of God with one more story. I will call it "The Brooms."

Many years ago, my husband decided to take part in an investment opportunity. This was years after I'd had my mystical experience. He found one that he liked, and it involved brooms. I was not sure about it and tried to discourage the idea, especially since the cost to us would be $6,000. To my dismay, the contract was signed, and soon our basement was filled with brooms.

His impression was that the brooms would be sold through large superstores. It turned out that the brooms went into small paint stores and such.

When it became apparent to us the brooms would not sell quickly, if at all, we were very discouraged. After a few weeks, the basement full of brooms caused me to go upstairs to weep over the loss of $6,000.

I stayed up there for a long time, filled with self-pity. Suddenly, through my crying, I felt I heard a voice. I had to stop crying in order to listen. The voice seemed to be the voice of Jesus. What I heard was, "This is only a material thing, and if you will let it go, I will be there for you when your life on earth is done. I will come and hold your hand."

I was not going to take any chances in wondering if this voice was only my imagination. I replied quickly, "Oh yes, Jesus, not only the $6,000, but if I had a million, I would give it to hold your hand."

As I said this, a wonderful feeling of peace came over me. I was completely happy. I ran downstairs, not caring if my husband would believe or not, that I heard the voice of Jesus. The brooms and money meant nothing to me now.

The next day, when my neighbor called on me to remind me of the Bible study we would soon be attending, she also inquired about the truck she had seen bringing in all the brooms. I invited her downstairs to see. After telling her my spiritual story of Jesus, I offered her a broom. She understood me completely and did not doubt my story.

The next day, I heard my husband talking to someone on the telephone. When he finished with the call, he said to me, "You will not believe this, but the company is giving us our money back. They will be coming tomorrow to get all of the brooms."

This was a shock to me. Now I would have the money and not Jesus. I stood there sadly wondering about the situation when I saw a vision of Jesus, smiling an amused smile at me. "Now you are going to have both!" he said. Giving up one thing will bring not less but more. I knew I had to tell others about the workings of God. He wants to give us everything. He loves us with an unending love.

When we attended the Bible study class, the instructor called for the new students to come up to the altar for the first hymn. My neighbor and I stood side by side up at the altar. When the hymn was announced, I noticed it was "What a Friend We Have in Jesus." As the congregation happily sang the hymn, I could not stop myself from crying. I cried through every verse. My understanding neighbor put her arm around me and held me.

The words of that song rang so true to me, I had just experienced the friendship of Jesus. Feeling foolish for crying through such a beautiful hymn, a line from the Bible came to me: "Be a fool for Christ."

I was happy to be just that.